# Mamita's House
## A True Tale of Tortilla Flat

Mamita's House is about an extended California Indian family that lived during the depression years in a neighborhood in Carmel, California called Tortilla Flat. It was to this neighborhood that John Steinbeck came to learn about the life of the *paisanos*. While Steinbeck used characters from Tortilla Flat in his book of that name, he told a different story from the equally compelling true one. The true one focuses on Mamita as a family heroine with the strength and fire to bring her family through tumultuous times. This account brings the reader an insight into the experience of California Indian People as they moved from tribal life to the urban life they have today. Recent photographs connect today's descendants with those who lived in and around Mamita's House at the turn of the last century.

Lois Robin

ISBN  1450546072

EAN 139781450546072

Primary Category Biography & Autobiography / Native Americans

**Robin Productions**

Santa Cruz, California, USA

## Other Works by Lois Robin

### Books
*Indian Ghosts at California Missions*
*The Butterflies of India: Women's Everyday Artistry*

### Photographic Exhibits
*A PhotoStudy for Peace*
*Flotsam and Jetsam*
*My Other Garden*
*Indian Ghosts at California Missions*
*We Are Still Here*

### Contributing Articles
*News from Native California:* "A Day with Diana"
*Encyclopedia of Birth Control:* "Native Americans of California"
*A Gathering of Voices:* "The Pajaro Valley Ohlone Indian Council"
*Journal of Great Basin Anthropology:* "I'm an Indian, but Who Am I?"

### Contributing Photographs
Time-Life Book, *The California Indian*
*Ocean's Festival Catalog*
*Discovery Works,* Houghton Mifflin text book
*El Andar,* "West Coast Tamalada"

### CD
*First People of the Pajaro*

### Videos
*A Song for the River*
*Stuck in the Mud: The Pajaro River in Peril*

### Exhibits Curated
*California's Sesquicentennial: An Indian Perspective*
*Rumme Living River: The Pajaro River Experience*

Photographic Website: LoisRobin.com

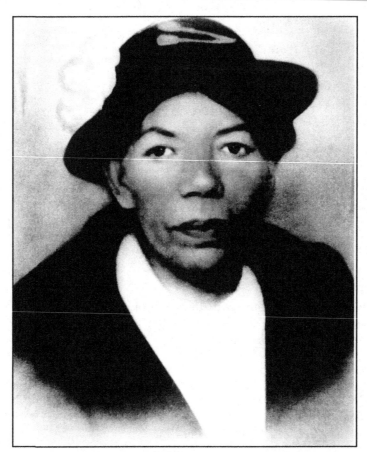

Mamita

# Mamita's House
## A True Tale of Tortilla Flat

As told by Lois Robin

Lovingly dedicated to

Jennifer Robin and Daniel Robin

of Lois' House

# Acknowledgments

Mamita's family, particularly Patrick Orozco, Terry Reynaga, Gloria Scott and Mary Ann Carbone, generously provided me with all the records they had of Mamita's life. They read and commented on the text, supplying anecdotes as they remembered them. Gloria Scott, Mamita's great-granddaughter who resembles Mamita, was an intuitive model. Her sister Mary Ann found reminiscent clothing for Gloria to wear.

Elizabeth Rondelle, present owner of Mamita's House, was gracious in allowing me to photograph Gloria in her home. Her father, John Logan, had kept an excellent record of letters he received from Mamita's family regarding genealogies and significant events in the history of the house. Although he is no longer here to thank, his careful records have made this work possible. I met John Logan once and was impressed with his lively humanity and orderly mind.

Others besides Mamita's descendants who read and commented on the story were my journalist sister, Julie Wheelock, publisher Malcolm Margolin, anthropologist Rob Edwards and Steinbeck scholar Audry Lynch. I am appreciative of the time they took and interest they showed.

Pat Hathaway of Monterey graciously consented to my using several photographs from his archives that bear his copyright.

Indispensable help with the InDesign program and book design suggestions came from the multi-talented Ann Pike.

Ted Orland, photography instructor at Cabrillo College and author, spurred the idea of publication and cheered me on.

Audry Lynch, a Steinbeck enthusiast and scholar, was confident of a place in the Steinbeck literature for this memoir. I have valued her friendship, support and acumen.

I will also be appreciative of those who, reading what I have written, send me other stories about Mamita's House that I can incorporate in another edition. I am sure there is more to tell, and I welcome all contributions.

Lois Robin
Santa Cruz, CA 95062
(831) 464--3939
robin@baymoon.com  www.loisrobin.com

# Contents

# Preface

My friend Patrick Orozco, a California Indian living in Watsonville, California, and I went one day to visit the house in Carmel where his great-grandmother Mamita used to live. At the time of our visit, the genial John Logan owned and lived in the house. John was a scholarly chronicler of local history. As I sat in the tiny living room, stories that Patrick had told me about his ancestry mingled with the questions and discoveries of John Logan, and my brain began to inhabit this house. Story and incident mingled and meshed, and I considered how I might one day tell this story that was coming alive in that moment. In this memoir, I combine image and narrative to tell about the amazing inhabitants of this house and the robust life that was lived in it. I am grateful to the descendents of Mamita who have encouraged me to tell her story. I am regretful that I do not know all the 275+ descendants for I am sure that many of them have compelling stories and information as well.

Some time ago, I met John Steinbeck's son Thom in a bookstore in Carmel where he was speaking about his recently published book. I said, "Thom, I know the true story of Tortilla Flat, and it is as fascinating as the one your father wrote. Would you be interested in writing it?" He said, "No, you write it." I demurred, "But I'm not a good enough writer." Smilingly he said, " You will be by the time you've finished it."

When a story needs telling, you don't really worry if you're a good enough writer, or not. You tell it.

Mamita's great–grandchild Gloria Scott welcomes us to to the House

# 1

## How Mamita's House came to be

**M**AMITA'S house still exists on Monterey Street and Second Avenue in Carmel, California, and you can see it rising above the fence. Now painted a cheery red and white, it has balconies, balustrades and a chimney.

The house in Mamita's day was a two story plain board and batten sitting on a mudsill foundation.

The story of Mamita's House is about the vibrant life in that house while Mamita lived in it and was mistress of it. It is about the difficulties and disasters, the calamities and limitations and how they were overcome and family life supported. The neighborhood was called Tortilla Flat, and Mamita's House was the center of life there.

Why was it called Tortilla Flat? One family story is that the house sat at the top of a hill that seemed flat after the steep road visitors took to get there. Mamita, being hospitable, used to offer her visitors coffee and tortillas after their arduous climb. Hence, Tortilla Flat.

The name Tortilla Flat is likely to bring to mind the book by John Steinbeck. *Tortilla Flat*, released in 1935, took the public and its author by surprise. It was Steinbeck's first great success and is a popular read today. It begins:

4

*Monterey sits on the slope of a hill, with a blue bay below it and with a forest of tall dark pine trees at its back. The lower parts of the town are inhabited by Americans, Italians, catchers and canners of fish. Behind the hill where the forest and town intermingle, where the streets are innocent of asphalt and the corners free of street lights, the old inhabitants of Monterey are as embattled as the Ancient Britons are embattled in Wales. These are the paisanos. They live in old wooden houses set in weedy yards, and the pine trees from the forest are about the houses.*

Mamita's house was nestled where forest and town intermingle, where the streets are innocent of asphalt. Today, that street has a rural look though it is paved.

Street in Tortilla Flat today

Steinbeck's book at first repelled the good citizens of Monterey for they did not want to hear about his paisanos and their antics, who were generally considered low life and immoral. Later the same citizens enthroned Steinbeck as local hero because of the popularity of the book and the tourists that came to the area hoping to locate the places he wrote about. Many people were curious about the location of Tortilla Flat and its characters.

Biographer Jackson Benson wrote:

> According to Charley Chaplin's son Charles Jr., his father was fascinated by Steinbeck's books and used to drive around the countryside where his stories were laid, trying to place the characters in the books in their proper locations.

Charley needed to search no farther than Mamita's house, for Steinbeck used to come to it to drink coffee and soak up the life there. Mamita's family remembers his frequent visits to their house.

In his book *The Intricate Music* John Kiernan writes:

> During John's residence in Pacific Grove the year before, he had met a young Monterey high school teacher named Susan Gregory. Sue Gregory was partly of Mexican descent and had cultivated a folkloric interest in Monterey's poor Mexican paisano population, most of whom lived in a community of shanties on a flat in the hills above the town. Because of its exclusively Mexican character, the community was called locally, and somewhat derisively, Tortilla Flat. Sue Gregory, an aspiring poet as well as a teacher, had managed to find in the poverty and illiteracy of the inhabitants of Tortilla Flat a dignity and humor that inspired her to write poems about them...

6

*Sue Gregory was to be his introduction to the people of Tortilla Flat, just as Ricketts had been his introduction to those of Cannery Row. Sue Gregory had taken John on several occasions into the flat and regaled him with stories about its inhabitants that underlined both their native dignity and their survival and humor in the face of adversity. John agreed that they would make interesting short story subjects.*

The biographer has it partially wrong. When John visited Mamita's House, he visited a Native American community who spoke Spanish, but for the most part were not Mexican. To what extent was Steinbeck influenced by the flavor of life there and the daily doings of its characters? *Tortilla Flat* is an imaginative comedic novel based on the Knights of the Round Table, an enticing theme to Steinbeck. Although his characters are based on the people he encountered in Tortilla Flat, he did not write their story. His story is about a group of ne'er-do-wells who came together around their leader Danny, had many escapades and misadventures and eventually came to understand the power of goodness and courage. Mamita did not have a round table, but a long rectangular one that she spread out in her living room. There she fed upwards of seventeen children usually in two shifts.

With Gloria we enter the house

This tiny living room once had a single large table where the family ate in two shifts.

The true story of Tortilla Flat would have been difficult to tell at the time it was unfolding. Life at Mamita's house was eventful, often painful. Only in retrospect is it possible to fathom how the disasters were overcome, the dangers met and the family survived. It was less complicated for Steinbeck to imagine fictional heroes than to navigate the unpredictable course of the real people at Tortilla Flat. Of course, fiction was his oeuvre and invention his gift. We would expect no less of him.

However, Mamita is a real hero, and her zest for life, compassion and resourcefulness dominate the real story, while the destructive behavior of many of those around her only attest to her strength under fire.

# 2

## How Mamita's House originated with Tio Bishi—her uncle

Mamita lived in the house from the turn of the twentieth century until 1939, when she lost the house for nonpayment of taxes. She was certainly in the house by 1900; her child Frederico was born there that year, and his birth certificate gives the address of the house. Her uncle, Luis Tarango, called Tio Bishi, owned the house at least from 1900, and he and his friends may have built it before then. Luis most likely encouraged Mamita to live in it to accommodate her burgeoning family. He was reputedly very fond of his niece. The house was still registered in his name in 1916. Sometime after that the house was deeded to Mamita.

# 3

## How Mamita had many husbands—legal & otherwise—& children

Mamita's first husband was Jose Cruz. He was stabbed in a fight and died at age 35 in December, 1896 from resultant gangrene. Her first daughter Irene was born in 1893 when Mamita was about 14 years old. Irene died giving birth in 1913.

Daughter Irena and husband Joe Williams, 1912

Teresa was born in 1897 and lived for many years until 1986, long after Mamita's death, retaining much family knowledge.

After Jose Cruz's death, Mamita partnered with Terso Marquez. She would live with him for twenty years until they separated. With Terso she had eight children: Angelina, Luis, Frederico, Minnie, Ignacia, Hermina, Henry and Terso Edward II. The last of these children to die was Minnie in 1974.

Daughter Minnie married William Marshall and they lived in an adjoining house known as the Minnie Marshall house.

Gloria in front of the Minnie Marshall House

Finally she married Martin Soto, who lived with her less time than Terso. Nevertheless, she had three children with him; the first, Rita died in childbirth, the second Carlotta died in 1975 and the third was Juanita "Jennie," also deceased. Martin's name is registered with hers on the house deed. For that reason the House is often referred to by historical societies as the Soto House when it isn't called by its descriptive name Old Timber.

Mamita died in 1941 when she was 64 years old. Martin lived for some time after that. It was said that the loss of the house contributed to Mamita's rapid decline. When she was unable to pay the taxes, a realtor Daisy Bostick took over the house in 1939 after paying the $100.00 owed in back taxes. She gave Mamita $10.00 as a consolation gift.

# 4

## How the House became the vessel for a legend

The house had 438 feet upstairs and 438 downstairs. The upstairs was one large bedroom.

Who knows how many slept upstairs in the bedroom? Mamita had a bed upstairs on the side near the steps. In summer the children were often bedded down outdoors in an old cart or a nearby garage.

The downstairs was divided into three rooms: kitchen, living room and dining room. The living room contained a very large table where the children used to eat in shifts. Sometimes family members ate outdoors where a large pot on a wood stove provided food throughout the day.

Gloria climbs the narrow steps to the upstairs where once all the children were bedded.

The yard was generous and must have existed in Mamita's day much as it does now, although then it had Indian tobacco (possibly curly dock, yerba santa or marijuana) growing in it that Mamita used regularly, wrapping the leaves in Bull Durham papers.

Mamita once stood at this window watching the children as they played outdoors.

Visitors have written that there were seldom fewer than seventeen children in the house; Mamita's own, those that her children left with her to raise and others that were just taken in. Luis Tarango and his wife left her a waif called Douglas to raise (who later became a millionaire). Mamita not only cooked and clothed these children but fostered their cultural knowledge with songs and stories. She told their fortunes with cards, calling it "El Suerte." She knew that spirit was as important as food in sustaining a family. Sometimes when enraged she would utter swear words in a language no one knew. The kitchen in Mamita's house is tiny. There is room for only one or two persons. Not only did Mamita cook there for the family, she also made tamales, a long process, to sell at the Carmel Mission.

Among the native dishes she prepared were *budia* (a drink made of acorns), *chwal* (similar to spinach), *panemi* (an acorn bread) and *pelili* (a fry bread stuffed with almost anything).

In this small kitchen Mamita prepared food for all.

Sometimes the children were asked to cruise the neighborhood, knock on doors and sell the tamales for a dime each. She made herbal salves and ointments there for her healing practice. She and others made food for fiestas and wakes in that kitchen.

Somehow she also found time to be a midwife to the many babies who came along and to the extended community.

Another way that Mamita supported her family was by making wreaths of redwood boughs at Christmas and selling them in the front of the Carmel post office. This activity became a family trademark and successive generations continued for many years to make and sell them.

Gloria inherits the family tradition.

The atmosphere in the house was hardly that of downtrodden and marginal people. They danced and partied. Celebrations were common at the house. Every Saturday there was a fiesta with a lot of drinking. Sometimes it got out of hand and there were fights. There was a sign that describd the general atmosphere:

# Old Soto House
## scene of great dancing, roistering & brawling

An outdoor deck (that no longer exists) was the probable site of many parties and festivities. There was also a platform to the south where dances took place. Many of the dances were Indian and followed proscribed patterns.

Sometimes sacred dances were conducted in distant places in nature. Annie Orozco, a grandchild, remembered going to such places.

At that dance, all the regalia was used, the language was still spoken and ceremonial songs were sung. The participants would begin in the early, early hours with an old Indian known as El Sordo (Juan Jose Barnebel).

The old Indian came to the house and one by one the other Indians would come to the meeting place at Mamita's house. The Indian would lead them to a trail into the mountains. It took hours and hours to get to their destination. According to Annie, when they reached this destination, there was an area that was like a little climb before an opening–the dancing area. She said the women would all go to the side and open their pouches. They would take out Indian instruments;

whistles, clapper sticks and others. The men would begin to put on dance regalia: animal skins and bird feathers. The women would start to sing and play their instruments and the men begin to dance. She said the area was scattered with different types of artifacts, which indicated it was a ceremonial site used for many years. The ceremonies were called "Jamikas." Sea gull eggs or eggs from any bird were used to make *harrikiyah*. Later chicken eggs were used. *Harrikiyah* was a type of mush made from eggs.

# 5

## How Mamita's Family came from San Buenaventura and brought Chumash Indian influence to Carmel

Who was she and how did she come to be a "paisano" at Tortilla Flat? Mamita was born Mary Dixon around 1877. Her mother was Maria Petra Tarango and of Indian descent. Her brother, Jose David Dixon, is a tragic figure in this story. Her father, David Dixon, was a Yankee, perhaps from Canada or England and some said from an army base. Some remembered him as white, some as black. He disappeared not too long after Mary was born. Petra seems to have disappeared early in Mamita's life (she died before 1900), and grandmother Maria Cano raised Mamita. They were most likely Chumash Indians who came from Ventura County to work in the New Idrea mines, settling eventually in Carmel. Petra's brother, already mentioned as the donor of the house, was Luis Tarango, called Tio Bishi (Little Squirrel) by the family. He was a well-respected person. At the age of 19 he was working as a miner at New Almaden. Ten years later in 1880, he was working at New Idria. By 1900 he was farming near Monterey and managed to accumulate considerable property in that area.

It is said that Maria Cano spoke four Indian languages: Seri, Yaqui, Opata and Ventureño. The first three are spoken in Sonora in Mexico. In that case perhaps Sonora was the ancestral home, and the family moved from Sonora to Ventura before heading towards Central California. No one has definitively fit this linguistic information into the rest of the family history. Recently, however, some Chumash descendants are bringing to light knowledge from their oral history that bears on this puzzle. During mission times, although some Chumash Indians went into the missions, others fled to Mexico. They stayed there for many generations until they felt safe to return once more to their ancestral homeland. Is it possible that this was the case with those who came before Mary Cano? Her family would have been able to return once the missions were desecularized by the Mexican government. The Seri language was spoken by Indians in Mexico who lived near the Pacific Ocean, their lifestyle similar to that of coastal California. Perhaps Mary Cano descended from Chumash ancestors who fled from the missions in the late 1700s, returning after 1833.

Mamita's half-brother, Edward Romandia, also a family member at Tortilla Flat, was listed on the Indian rolls of 1929 as a Chumash Indian. Written knowledge of the lineage goes back no further than Maria Cano. Gloria's family has heard that Maria Cano's ancestors came from a village called Halo near the coast in Santa Barbara. Although there was a town called Halo, the family's location at this site cannot be verified through records. Her birth certificate has not yet been located possibly because Cano may not have been the only name she used. It is likely that at some time family members were affiliated with the mission at San Buenaventura. Mamita was strongly connected to the Carmel Mission suggesting some prior family relationship with the missions. The Carmel Mission employed her as a cook on feast days. The family's blending of Catholicism with Indian beliefs also suggests, but does not confirm, a prior connection with the missions.

What is certain is that the family followed Indian ways and customs. They used Indian names for foods, sayings and celebration though Spanish was spoken most of the time. They honored the sacred. Mamita has at last count 275 descendants. Those who knew of her still revere her memory.

Steinbeck writes:

> What is a paisano? He is a mixture of Spanish, Indian, Mexican and assorted Caucasian bloods. His ancestors have lived in California for a hundred or two years... He is a paisano, and he lives in that uphill district above the town of Monterey called Tortilla Flat, although it isn't a flat at all.

Steinbeck acknowledges Indian influences, which he could not have missed if he spent much time in Tortilla Flat. But both he and his biographers write most often about the Mexican nature of the paisanos.

Steinbeck was either tongue in cheek or held the same uninformed opinion of Indians as the general population of that era, when he wrote of the Salinas Valley in *East of Eden*:

> First there were Indians, an inferior breed without energy, inventiveness, or culture, a people that lived on grub and grasshoppers and shellfish too lazy to hunt or fish. They ate what they could pick up and planted nothing. They pounded bitter acorns for flour. Even their warfare was a weary pantomime.

He then writes the place names the Spanish gave us from names of saints, or descriptions of places or names of animals. Missing are any of the numerous Indian place names. There was then a dearth of information about California Indians which has given way to a new appreciation and admiration of their culture; sensitive tending of the land, capacity to settle differences amicably, extensive cosmological knowledge and ingenious technology for hunting and fishing.

Mamita and her family were Native Americans. Their heritage was most likely that of the Chumash Indians of Ventura and Santa Barbara. And native influences dominated the stories and songs Mamita told the children and the dances held at the house and wilderness locations. It dominated life at Tortilla Flat and still influences most of Mamita's 275+ descendants. Yet outsiders, such as Steinbeck and his biographers, overlook this historical significance in their writings.

In the early twentieth century, when Mamita's family was located in Tortilla Flat, Indian people were outcasts. Being an indigenous Californian had no cachet at that time although that has now changed. For self-protection Indians had to deny their Indian affiliation to the outside world, and sometimes the denial pervaded their personal identity. The economy was depressed and Indians were marginalized in Carmel society. In the minds of most, the California Indians were extinguished, not distinguished. Little was understood of the rich culture of the neighboring Chumash, Ohlone, Esselen or Salinan. Mamita's descendants today honor their heritage in many ways and continue to be influenced by it. But then they were without status.

In the aftermath of California's mission era many of the Indian people who had once been affiliated with the missions continued that affiliation while other disavowed it. Mamita seems to have found a welcome berth in the Carmel Mission. She was employed by the Mission to cook for them on feast days and often sold tamales there.

Gloria remembering how Mamita used to sell tamales at the Mission. Here she is outside the bell tower, where Mamita and her kin would ring the bell.

Mamita is attending the cornerstone laying of a new room at the Carmel Basilica with other distinguished members of the Carmel mission and community. Her spouse Martin Soto is third from the right. Luis Tarango is second from the right. Her daughter Minnie Marshall stands on her right side. Manuel Onésimo (left) and another unknown Onesimo carry the cornerstone. Mission Curator Harry Downey is at the extreme right.

Photo from the Hathaway archive

# 6

## How the Rumor circulated about Tio Bishi was probably true

Tiburcio Vasquez, sire of Tio Bishi

Tio Bishi, Luis Tarango, uncle of Mamita

A rumor has persisted about the origins of Tio Bishi, Luis Tarango. A native woman who lived in the area, Isabel Meadows, told the anthropologist J.P. Harrington that Maria Cano, mother of Luis and Petra, said confidentially that the true father of Luis was Tiburcio Vasquez, the notorious bandit hanged for his crimes in San Jose in 1875. According to the confidentiality, Tiburcio, while in hiding from the law, stopped one night at Maria Cano's and was intimate with her.

In Harrington's notes Isabel frequently brings up this information. She notes the similarity in appearance between father and son although Tiburcio had an eye that did not function properly while Luis did not, she says. Luis was known by the family to have brought Tiburcio the clothes he wore for his hanging, and private correspondence shows the relationship between the two. Family members generally accept this information, and Tiburcio has found his way into their legend. Tiburcio, a lady's man as well as a bandit, is intriguing, and his fortunes and misfortunes have been used as the basis for stage plays and historical accounts. Historical places, such as Vasquez Rocks, (where he hid out) have been named for him. The difference in fate and fortune of sire and son is noteworthy, the father being hanged for misdeeds (which he claimed were a misunderstanding); the son, a pillar of the community. Of course Luis was not raised by Tiburcio but by his stepfather, Dolores Tarango.

Mamita's descendants see Tiburcio as a kind of Robin Hood who stole from the outside world but gave to the family. Consider Tiburcio's statement before his hanging.

> *A spirit of hatred and revenge took possession of me. I had numerous fights in defense of what I believed to be my rights and those of my countrymen. I believed we were unjustly deprived of the social rights that belonged to us.*

# 7

## How an anthropologist's notes and the recollections of a Rumsien Ohlone woman enter the story

Isabel Meadows and Brother Tom

Harrington's notes are handwritten in colloquial Spanish, English and Rumsien Ohlone. He interviewed Isabel as the last speaker of Rumsien. These notes are fragmentary and have never been completely translated. He is the filter for Isabel Meadows' comments. Isabel lived near Tortilla Flat, if not in it, and she was very forthcoming with what she knew of local people although she occasionally contradicted herself or was inaccurate. She used a disparaging tone when she talked about Mamita and her kin. She herself lived a quiet life with her brother and did not have a husband or children. Before she died at 94 years old, she provided the Smithsonian in Washington with the Rumsien language.

Harrington reports that:

> Iz [as he refers to her] feels sorry at times to recall how she never went to parties and was never wild like the other girls, but they are every one dead now, and she is still with us, 84 years old. [She lived another ten years.]

Isabel says throughout the Harrington notes that Luis Tarango came from San Buenaventura. For example:

> Luis Tarango was born at San Buenaventura evidently but was brought to Carmelo when a little boy.

Iz tells how her friend Ularia lost her life at the hands of Mamita.

> Ularia died neglected and full of piojos [lice] at her house at the Rancheria. Maria Tarango (she is the sister of Luis Tarango, she is the woman JP Harrington knows as Maria Soto) was responsible for Ularia's death. Maria was andando de mecha and stopped with Ularia just to sleep or to eat off of her, and Maria was heating a dishpan to wash the dishes, and went outdoors, and the water in the dishpan got to boiling and Ularia tried to set it off the stove and spilled it all over herself, scalding herself badly. They say she got pizanos [blackened skin] in her hands where the scald was. She lasted barely 3 weeks after getting scalded.

29

*August 1934. The Maria Tarango bunch at the beginning of July, when the soyosos [huckleberries] got ripe used to go with all the children gathering them to make a little money for buying clothes for the kids to wear to school in the fall... The daughters were so bad, they all brought home bastard kids for Maria to raise.*

*I used to like the soyosos and also the pie. It has a good taste, also good jelly.*

*Maria Tarango and all the banditos who were able to join them went out to pick soyosos. Lea Laura would always buy them. But when they had stolen the wood Alefonso was cutting, Ali told Laura not to buy any more from them.*

*The putas [whores] go to every wake, no mas de lambeones [beg?] to talk with the men and eat good. You always used to see them at wakes. How Maria Dixon came, was present day after day at Asc's wake.*

And she imparted healing advice recommended by Mamita's kin.

*Unto sin sal is a piece of fat that grows by the kidney of a mountain lion (or pig), you cut it and take the fat out, and it is a pure ointment. You can also melt it in the sarten [frying pan] with some camphor to make it a stronger ointment.*

Mamita, posing gracefully, is upper top right. Her daughter Irena is center with the goat. All but the friend on the left are Mamita's children. No one seems to know how the goat figured in the story, but the picture is known as the "goat" picture.

# 8

## How other characters from the Flats came into Steinbeck's novel

El Sordo, the likely model for Steinbeck's Pirate

Photo from the Hathaway archive

Another denizen of the Flats was a very old Indian named El Sordo. He was most likely the inspiration for the Pirate in Steinbeck's book. But El Sordo was so named because he was deaf, the deaf one, while Steinbeck's character was short on intellect. El Sordo's true name was Juan Jose Bernabe, or Barnabel, and he was probably raised by the distinguished Indian Onésimo family. Like Steinbeck's character, he had a dog Bull who was his pack, going with him wherever he went. He was fierce in protecting this animal. He picked up wood on a wheelbarrow or wagon and sold it for small amounts of money. Picking and selling huckleberries produced other income. He may have had a small military pension. Obsessed with buried treasure, he was afraid the children would discover what he had buried. As his health deteriorated, Mamita had him live in a trailer near her house. He scared some children and impressed others as being kind, often bringing food and candies to them. He frequently "baby sat" at the house but snitched to Mamita on indiscretions of the children. Apparently he knew much about Indian dance and ceremony, living to the age of 104 to share his knowledge.

Barnabe in his own way was legendary. He used to carve animals on a tree near the cabin where he lived in Hatton Canyon. The carvings eventually disappeared, but that spot today is a perpetual altar where people come to meditate. In Steinbeck's book, Pirate has a religious experience in the mission. A spiritual quality illumines both the real and fictional characters.

From *Tortilla Flat*:

> *A great many people saw the Pirate every day, and some laughed at him, and some pitied him; but no one knew him very well, and no one interfered with him. He was a huge, broad man, with a tremendous black and bushy beard. He wore jeans and a blue shirt, and he had no hat. In town he wore shoes. There was a shrinking in the Pirate's eyes when he confronted any grown person, the secret look of an animal that would like to run away if it dared turn its back long enough. Because of this expression, the paisanos of Monterey knew that his head had not grown up with the rest of his body. They called him The Pirate because of his beard. Every day people saw him wheeling his barrow of pitch wood about the streets until he sold the load. And always in a cluster at his feet walked his five dogs.*
>
> *The Pirate lived in a deserted chicken house in the yard in a deserted house on Tortilla Flat. He would have thought it presumptuous to live in the house itself. The dogs lived around and on top of him, and the Pirate liked this, for his dogs kept him warm on the coldest nights.*

Another major character in Steinbeck's book, the person well informed on every topic of importance to Danny's gang, was Pilon, based on real life Eddie Ramirez, who lived in a cave and was a frequent visitor at Tortilla Flat.

Steinbeck writes ironically of Pilon:

> Pilon was a lover of beauty and a mystic. He raised his face into the sky and his soul arose out of him into the sun's afterglow. That not too perfect Pilon, who plotted and fought, who drank and cursed, trudged slowly on; but a wistful and shining Pilon went up to the sea gulls where they bathed on sensitive wings in the evening. That Pilon was beautiful, and his thoughts were unstained with selfishness and lust. And his thoughts are good to know.

In the words of biographer Jackson Benson:

> The most notorious of these men in life, Pilon (Eddie Ramirez) has left a legacy of legend that has made him a sort of folk hero (a back-handed fulfillment of Steinbeck's prophecy in the novel that Danny would become the subject of a myth). Part of the time, he and a friend, Edy Martin, lived in a cave in Iris Canyon, twenty feet up the bank, which they called their summer home; Pilon called the county farm his "rest home" and went there regularly to dry out.

Another personality who often participated in the fiestas and gatherings at Tortilla Flat was a woman named Flora Woods. Steinbeck writes about her in *Cannery Row*, only her fictitious name was Dora Flood. Neither Steinbeck nor his biographers mention that she was Indian in background and for that reason was drawn to activities at Tortilla Flat.

Young............ and old  Flora-Dora                By John Thompson

*On the left of the lot is the stern and stately whorehouse of Dora Flood, a decent clean, honest, old-fashioned sporting house where a man can take a glass of beer among friends. This is no fly-by-night cheap clip joint but a sturdy, virtuous club, built, maintained, and disciplined by Dora, who, madam and girl for fifty years, has through the exercise of special gifts of tact and honesty, charity and a certain realism, made herself respected by the intelligent, the learned, and the kind... Dora is a great big woman with flaming orange hair and a taste for Nile green evening dresses.*

The family remembers Flora Woods leaving generous tips under her plate for the servers at the Tortilla Flat fiestas.

From an illustration by Peggy Worthington in the 1947 edition of *Tortilla Flat*

### Was Mamita the inspiration for any of Steinbeck's characters?

Steinbeck's biographers do not specify her likeness to any of the book's female personalities. But in the sheer number of her children she is reminiscent of Senora Teresina Cortez.

> *Senora Teresina Cortez and her eight children and her ancient mother lived in a pleasant cottage on the edge of the deep gulch that defines the southern frontier of Tortilla Flat. Teresina was a good figure if a mature woman nearing thirty. Her mother, that ancient, dried, toothless one, relict of a past generation, was nearly fifty. It was long since any one had remembered that her name was Angelica.*

*During the week work was ready to this vieja's hand, for it was her duty to feed, punish, cajole, dress and bed down seven of the eight children. Teresina was busy with the eighth, and with making certain preparations for the ninth.*

*On Sunday, however, the vieja, clad in black satin more ancient even than she, hatted in a grim and durable affair of black straw, on which were fastened two true cherries of enameled plaster, threw duty to the wind and went firmly to church, where she sat as motionless as the saints in their niches. Once a month, in the afternoon, she went to confession. It would be interesting to know what sins she confessed, and where she found the time to commit them, for in Teresina's house there were* **creepers, crawlers, stumblers, shriekers, cat-killers, fallers-out-of-trees,** *and each one of these charges could be trusted to be ravenous every two hours.*

Steinbeck takes a comedic stance on these children and also on Senora Teresina.

*Teresina was a mildly puzzled woman, as far as her mind was concerned. Her body was one of those perfect retorts for the distillation of children. The first baby, conceived when she was 14, had been a shock to her... The regularity with which she became a mother always astonished Teresa. It occurred sometimes that she could not remember who the father of the impending baby was; and occasionally she almost grew convinced that no lover was necessary. In the time when she had been under quarantine as a diphtheria carrier, she conceived just the same.*

The general outline of a woman who bore many children and raised them may have been modeled on Mamita, who had her first child at fourteen years, but the Mamita of our legend was an authoritative woman who welcomed children and raised them with deep caring and resourcefulness.

# 9

## How beans reveal much about the Family's lifestyle

In the novel, the beans consumed by the family are in short supply, and the school personnel are chagrined that the children, though apparently healthy, eat nothing but beans. Danny and his friends attempt a remedy by bringing Teresina vegetables, fish and meat which rot on her porch until Teresina begs them to remove their gifts, saying her kids can only be healthy on beans. Eventually the heroic troubadours conspire to bring her large sacks of beans. In real life a more likely scenario, according to those who remember, is that Mamita would distract the truck drivers who came through while the children would pilfer vegetables off their trucks. The members of the family were ingenious at finding food. The men knew how to hunt, kill and dress game animals. They knew places in the wild to find berries. But there must have been seasons of the year when additional produce was needed. And the provident Mamita knew how to get it. She knew her family needed other foods than beans to thrive.

Old family photo shows David as a teenager, playing accordion

# 10

## How members of the Family fared well...or ill

Mamita's brother David Dixon is shown in several pictures playing the accordion. There was always music at the house. On the Saturday night fiestas David was the accordionist while Terso II played the guitar. The photo shows him as a teenager, playing accordion.

No. 12379
Name David Tarango
County Monterey
Crime Aslt to Murder & Prior
Term 14 Years
Received 3/29/13

But all was not well with David. He became an alcoholic or perhaps, according to some accounts, he was mentally unstable.

He was in jail four times for serious offenses. His face in this jail mug shot reveals a man in deep pain. At one time, while Martin Soto was Mamita's partner, David seriously threatened the family's welfare. On Mamita's orders Martin Soto shot David with a rifle and killed him.

The murder was ruled justifiable homicide. The sheriff, Gus Englund, knew of the threat and was coming to stop David, but his timing was off and David's behavior was menacing. We can only guess about Mamita's grief with this incident.

After he died in 1924 his personal property was burned next to the house. Burning the remains of the deceased was a practice of most California Indian People.

Angelina, Mamita's first born with Terso Marquez, was probably between partners when she left her daughter Frances for Mamita to raise. After much anguish over the loss of a mother who would never return as promised, Frances bonded with her grandmother and later raised thirteen children of her own much as Mamita raised her.

Frances had many stories to tell her own daughters about life at Mamita's house. Her daughters Gloria, Arlene, Mary Ann and Sheena have all heard about great-grandmother. When asked if it was all right to write about some family members still alive, they agreed: "Our mother Frances told us to tell the truth. We must never be afraid of the truth."

Frances' first child, which she had when she was fourteen years old, was the result of a rape by Martin Soto, her step-grandfather. Martin went to jail for the rape. The child thrived. Frances had claim to some of Mamita's strength. Still a teenager, she served jail time, taking a rap for her reckless brothers. She had her first baby with her for a while in jail but was crushed when the authorities said the child had to leave because he had committed no crime.

Mamita with baby Frances

One of her daughters, Mary Ann Carbone, is today Vice Mayor of Sand City, working on community issues and taking an interest in Indian cultural affairs, a "can do" sort of person. Gloria, our guide, who resembles Mamita, works fulltime at a Safeway bakery and caretakes her grandchild when not working. Both have been helpful in providing recollections of Mamita that their mother passed on to them.

The home of some of Frances' children in Seaside resembles Mamita's house with family members trooping in and out with children and grandchildren and a pot of soup always available on the stove.

With Terso, Mamita had a son named Luis. Luis Marquez lived with his wife, Rose Rios, in a house in Tortilla Flat near Mamita. Luis and Rosa had a daughter Annie, who knew grandma Mamita as a young girl and relayed stories about her to her son, Patrick Orozco. Patrick was born in 1939, two years before Mamita's death at the time she was forced to sell her house. Patrick's mother reported that Mamita said, "This is the one who will bring it all back." And by that she meant the Indian culture and history. Indeed, Patrick was destined to "bring it all back" and has chronicled and documented the family history extensively. Patrick's knowledge from his mother Annie and his grandmother Rosa Rios contribute to the story of Mamita's House. Mamita comes to him in reflective moments as a dream guide.

Patrick described his grandfather, Luis Marquez, Mamita's son: "My grandfather was a strong, vital person and wonderfully kind. Yet, he drank seriously and heavily. Many years before I was born, he was a bootlegger. I remember his disinterest in money. He would throw a handful of coins into the air and not bother to pick them up. I used to check in with him when he was drunk or sober to see how he was doing. Even after my grandmother (Rosa Rios) remarried, Luis used to hang out at her place. All three of them got along well: Grandma, her second husband and Luis."

Some say that Mamita asked her daughter-in-law Rosa Rios to take care of her alcoholic son after she was gone, and that's why Luis continued to live with Rosa even after she remarried. Mamita had repeatedly bailed Luis out of jail when he was incarcerated for drunkenness. Although Luis was considered to be a kind, loving person, his reputation was stained by several incidences. Reputedly, he cut off the nose of Fermin Garcia, and on another occasion he shot and crippled his wife Rosa for her purported infidelity. She was confined to a wheel chair the rest of her life. The alcoholism in the family has been a curse, one that Patrick has tried to remedy in whatever way he can.

Drinking is not tolerated at the Gathering of the Elders or other tribal events held today.

In Steinbeck's book, the drinking of gallons of wine is playful, humorous, the blood of life. In the real family of Mamita's House, it was deadly.

The men of the family had long been separated from tribal roles. With little formal education, generally dispossessed in the society during economically depressed times, alcohol was a dangerous but real comfort. In the words of Mary Ann Carbone, "The men had nowhere to go."

Many descendants of Mamita, having escaped alcoholism and life threatening conditions, are leading gratifying lives. With each generation there is assimilation into the larger culture for employment, social status and education. At the same times, there is a return to the ancient cultural heritage and a push for equal rights and protection of the burials.

# 11

## How the support and love of Mamita was transferred to those she cared for

A Navajo social worker wrote the family her appreciation of their mother Frances:

> 1 wanted to let you know that your mother was a very special mother. Her heart was filled with pride because of her many children. She had many moments that were precious to her that touched her heart and mind, her many stories of what each of you had told her from your daily activities to your dreams. She treasured them and shared only a few of them with people whom she wanted to know of her children. Her glowing smile and heart always appeared in mentioning her family.

*She was proud to say that her children were not afraid of hard work and that it does pay. She demonstrated and shared it with all of her children at one time or another. She didn't have to put her head down, but held it high.*

*She mentioned a story of the Pelican that was told to her by her people. And tales of the sea giving food to your people... the many reasons of the sea's gift to your people: in making jewelry, trading shells for serving or other usage. The sand even gave of itself to help clean, make things... and the list went on. She often wondered if you might remember some of the stories... she spoke of the sea horses that came and showed themselves to your people with song and stories. Good times and scary, but still interesting.*

*Your mother had a lot of history, and I don't know if anyone had recalled or repeated them or put them in written form. She was a very remarkable woman. She was a strong person when approached with her heritage. She didn't boast, but she was proud.*

*Her virtue was to say that her people were kind hearted, knowledgeable, valued family and acknowledged other native people's ways.*

*Your mother always encouraged reading; she tried to do so because of her limited educational background. She never feared to ask questions or question what was going on in the situation. Being a people person, she enjoyed being a Certified Nurse's Aide. She knew a lot of people from all ranges of race and beliefs. She treated people like she wanted to be treated.*

*She looked toward the bright side or saw that things happen for a good reason.*

*She demonstrated her skills for what was and for what she wanted to pass on to the family. She was proud of you and what you can become. She saw this potential in each of you. The stability was there, and she worked hard for it.*

*I was very blessed in knowing her and being able to listen to her comments on her life, heritage, language and beliefs. She told me that she prayed a lot to our Creator. She acknowledged that one needs spirit, health and family.*

*I hope this letter encourages some of your family members and yourself to write down your thoughts of your mother.*

Sonia Wapato Van Woerkom

Frances, having learned to deal with life from Mamita, had come through early rejection by her mother, teenage rape and pregnancy, false imprisonment and separation from her first baby with a positive outlook and the capacity for a richly rewarding life. Her marriage to a loving husband helped provide her with the sense of belonging and family she craved. Both Frances and her grandmother were resilient, spirited women.

# 12

## How Steinbeck summarizes Danny's House in his novel and how Mamita's House was in its own way similar

*This is the story of Danny and of Danny's friends and of Danny's house. It is a story of how these three became one thing, so that in Tortilla Flat if you speak of Danny's house you do not mean a structure of wood flaked with old whitewash, overgrown with an ancient untrimmed rose of Castile. No, when you speak of Danny's house you are understood to mean a unit of which the parts are men, from which came sweetness and joy, philanthropy and in the end, a mystic sorrow. For Danny's house was not unlike the Round Table, and Danny's friends were not unlike the knights of it. And this is the story of how that group came into being, of how it flourished and grew to be an organization beautiful and wise.*

This is the story of Mamita's House and from it came sweetness and joy, philanthropy and in the end a mystic sorrow. And this is the story of how that family came into being, of how it flourished and grew to be an organization beautiful and wise.

Perhaps John Steinbeck, sitting there in Mamita's House sipping coffee, was soaking up the spirit, humor and vitality of those who lived in Tortilla Flat, and did, after all, put their essence in his work.

Many will revisit Mamita's House with stories of their own
and a fresh sense of the valor and courage of its mistress.

But for now Gloria closes the door.

Made in the USA
Monee, IL
11 July 2020